RICH &

YOUNG

In 5 Steps

Unlocking the Secrets to Building Wealth and Success Early in Life

Introduction

Welcome to "Rich & Young" – the ultimate guide to achieving financial success at a young age. This book is for anyone who's tired of waiting until they're older to create the life they want, and who's ready to take control of their financial future right now.

You might be a student, a recent graduate, or just someone who's always felt like financial success was out of reach. You might feel like you don't have the right connections, or the right education, or the right experience to make it happen. But I'm here to tell you that none of that matters.

In "Rich and Young," I share practical advice, and expert insights to help you achieve your financial success.

In this book I will show you that it's possible to build wealth and create the life you want at any age – as long as you're willing to put in the work.

But "Rich & Young" is more than just a collection of inspiring stories. It's also a practical guidebook that will give you the tools and knowledge you need to start building your own wealth today. I share expert insights and advice on topics such as investing, budgeting, entrepreneurship, "Tricks and tips" and more, all tailored specifically to young people.

You'll learn how to identify your strengths and passions, and turn them into profitable ventures. You'll discover the secrets of successful investing, and how to make your money work for you. And you'll learn how to overcome the common challenges and obstacles that young people face when trying to achieve financial success.

Ultimately, "Rich & Young" is about empowering you to take control of your financial future and create the life you want – not someday, but right now. So if you're ready to start building wealth and living life on your own terms, this book is for you. **Let's get started!**

Index

I'll be outlining a five-step process that you can follow to build wealth and achieve financial success while you're still young.

STEP 1

Start by yourself first

Know yourself:

Knowing and understanding oneself is a crucial aspect of personal development that can help you become more self-aware, confident, and fulfilled. By getting to know yourself better, you can identify your passions, strengths, and values, and develop a sense of purpose and direction in life.

You can also become more aware of your weaknesses and areas for improvement, allowing you to work on these areas and become a better version of yourself.

Once you have identified your strengths, weaknesses, and faults, the next step is to work on them to improve your overall well-being and success.

Remember that improving your qualities and faults is a lifelong process that requires ongoing effort and commitment. With dedication and a willingness to learn and grow, you can become the best version of yourself and achieve greater success and fulfillment in all areas of your life.

Be comfortable with yourself:

Feeling good about who you are as a person, both on the inside and the outside. It's about accepting your strengths and weaknesses, and being confident in your own skin.

When you're comfortable with yourself, you don't worry too much about what other people think of you. You're able to be yourself without pretending to be someone you're not, and you don't feel the need to impress others or seek validation from them. You know your own worth and you trust yourself to make decisions that are right for you.

Being comfortable with yourself also means taking care of your physical and mental health, but not obsessing over your appearance or body image. It means being kind to yourself when things don't go as planned, and not beating yourself up over mistakes or setbacks.

It takes time and effort to become comfortable with yourself, but it's worth it. By practicing self-awareness, self-acceptance, and self-compassion, you can develop a stronger sense of self and live a more fulfilling life.

Self-reflection and introspection:

Self-reflection and introspection are processes of examining one's thoughts, feelings, and experiences to gain a deeper understanding of oneself. Both involve looking inward and exploring one's inner world, including beliefs, values, strengths, weaknesses, and emotions.

Self-reflection typically involves contemplation, evaluation, and analysis of one's experiences and thoughts. It can be done in a structured way, such as through journaling, or informally through introspection.

Introspection, on the other hand, involves a more spontaneous and immediate examination of one's thoughts and emotions. It often involves paying attention to one's internal experiences and reflecting on them in the moment.

Both self-reflection and introspection are valuable tools for personal growth and self-awareness. They can help in gaining insights into one's patterns of behavior, decision-making, and emotional responses, which can be used to make positive changes in one's life.

Invest in yourself

Investing in yourself means taking care of your personal and professional development by learning new things, developing new skills, and taking care of your physical and mental health. It's about making an effort to grow and improve yourself to achieve your goals.

For example, investing in yourself can mean taking a course to learn a new skill, joining a gym or practicing yoga to improve your physical health, or taking up a new hobby that enriches your life. It can also mean spending time with people who inspire and challenge you, or volunteering for a cause that you care about.

Investing in yourself is important because it helps you to become the best version of yourself. It can help you to be more successful in your career, and also to be more fulfilled in your personal life. By investing in yourself, you are making a commitment to your growth and development, which can lead to a more fulfilling and meaningful life.

Emotional self-control:

The first block or step towards building wealth is Emotional self-control.

When it comes to building wealth, emotional self-control is first, because it lays the foundation for all other financial success.

Without emotional self-control, it's easy to become overwhelmed by fear, greed, and other emotions that can lead to irrational decisions and impulsive behaviors. These decisions can be detrimental to your financial goals, causing setbacks and even failure.

On the other hand, when you develop emotional self-control, you are better equipped to make rational decisions based on sound financial principles. You are more likely to resist the temptation to overspend, make risky investments, or give in to other impulsive behaviors that can hinder your wealth-building efforts.

Emotional self-control is also important because it can help you maintain a positive mindset and stay focused on your long-term financial goals, even in the face of challenges and setbacks. It can help you navigate financial stresses and pressures with grace and resilience, and allow you to bounce back from setbacks more quickly.

Focusing on emotional self-control is a smart approach when it comes to building wealth, as emotions can often lead us to make irrational decisions when it comes to money.

Tips on how to develop emotional self-control:

Practice mindfulness: Mindfulness is the practice of being fully present and aware of your thoughts and emotions in the moment. By practicing mindfulness regularly, you can become more aware of your emotional triggers and learn to regulate your responses.

Identify your emotional triggers: Take some time to reflect on what situations or events tend to trigger emotional responses in you. Once you have identified your triggers, you can begin to develop strategies to manage them.

Develop a plan for managing emotions: Create a plan for how you will manage your emotions when they arise. This could involve taking a few deep breaths, going for a walk, or talking to a trusted friend or family member.

Take a long-term perspective: When it comes to building wealth, it's important to take a long-term perspective and avoid making impulsive decisions based on short-term emotions. Remind yourself of your long-term goals and focus on making decisions that align with those goals.

Seek support: Building emotional self-control takes time and practice, so don't be afraid to seek support from a coach, therapist, or mentor who can help you develop the skills you need to manage your emotions and build wealth.

Self-discipline:

Self-discipline is the ability to control your actions, thoughts, and emotions to reach your goals. It means making a conscious effort to stay focused and motivated, even when you face distractions or challenges that make you want to quit.

Being self-disciplined can help you in many ways. For example, it can improve your productivity, help you manage your time better, and allow you to make better decisions that lead to long-term success. It can also help you control your emotions and reactions, which can lead to greater resilience and overall well-being.

Developing self-discipline takes practice, and it can be challenging at times. However, setting clear goals, making a plan, and committing to following through with that plan can help you develop this valuable skill. With self-discipline, you can overcome obstacles, achieve your goals, and live a more fulfilling life.

Benefits of self-discipline:

Improved productivity: Self-discipline can help individuals stay focused and motivated, which can improve productivity and performance in various areas of life, including work, academics, and personal goals.

Better time management: Self-discipline can help individuals prioritize tasks, avoid procrastination, and manage time effectively, which can lead to greater productivity and less stress.

Increased self-control: Self-discipline can help individuals resist immediate gratification and make decisions based on long-term goals, which can lead to better outcomes and greater success.

Greater emotional resilience: Self-discipline can help individuals manage their emotions and reactions in challenging situations, which can improve emotional resilience and coping skills.

Improved health and wellness: Self-discipline can help individuals make healthy choices, such as exercising regularly, eating a balanced diet, and getting enough sleep, which can lead to better physical and mental health.

Behaviour and attitude:

Behavioral and attitude issues can have a significant impact on one's success in various areas of life, including personal relationships, academic pursuits, wealth, professional goals.

For instance, positive attitudes such as optimism, self-confidence, and resilience can enhance a person's ability to succeed. These attitudes can lead to productive behaviors, such as setting goals, taking risks, and persisting through challenges, which can help a person achieve their desired outcomes.

On the other hand, negative attitudes such as pessimism, self-doubt, and fear of failure can hinder a person's ability to achieve their desired outcomes. These attitudes can lead to self-sabotaging behaviors, such as procrastination, avoidance, and self-criticism, which can prevent a person from taking action towards their goals.

In addition, certain behavioral issues, such as impulsivity, lack of self-control, and poor communication skills, can also impact one's success. For example, if a person struggles with impulse control, they may make hasty decisions that have negative consequences. If a person has poor communication skills, they may struggle to build positive relationships or convey their ideas effectively in a professional setting.

Lifestyle and setting goals:

Finding your ideal lifestyle and setting goals can be a personal journey of self-discovery. You can start by taking some time to reflect on what matters most to you in life. Think about the things that bring you joy, fulfillment, and a sense of purpose. This can help you to identify the kind of lifestyle that aligns with your values and aspirations.

Once you have a general idea of what you want, you can start to imagine what your ideal lifestyle would look like. This is where you get to dream big and visualize yourself living the life you truly want. Think about where you want to live, what kind of job you want to have, the people you want to surround yourself with, and the experiences you want to have. This can help you to set specific goals that are meaningful and relevant to your overall vision.

When setting your goals, it's important to be realistic and break them down into achievable steps. This can help you to stay motivated and track your progress along the way. Prioritizing your goals based on their importance can also help you to stay focused and allocate your time and energy effectively.

Taking action towards your goals is key to making them a reality. This can involve small steps that add up over time, such as learning a new skill, networking with people in your field, or saving money towards a specific goal. The important thing is to take consistent action and keep moving forward, even when faced with setbacks or challenges.

Finding your ideal lifestyle and setting goals is a process that takes time, patience, and self-compassion. Don't be afraid to experiment, make mistakes, and adjust your course as you go. By staying true to yourself and taking action towards the life you want, you can create a fulfilling and meaningful life that aligns with your values and aspirations.

Take the time to figure out what you really like and what your goals and objectives are! It's not always easy to know what we want in life, so this is a great step forward. By working on your self-control and obtaining self-discipline, you've also taken another important step towards achieving your goals.

Now it's time to focus on developing the skills and talents that will help you get to where you want to be in life. This could mean taking classes or workshops, reading books, or seeking out mentors or coaches to help you develop the skills you need. By investing in yourself in this way, you'll be better equipped to achieve the lifestyle and goals you want for yourself.

Success doesn't happen overnight, but by taking consistent action towards your goals, you'll be well on your way to achieving the life you want. Keep pushing yourself to learn and grow, and stay focused on your objectives. With dedication and hard work, you can make your dreams a reality.

Congratulations on completing Step 1

Focusing on knowing yourself, being comfortable with yourself, investing in yourself, and determining your objectives and lifestyle at a young age can have a huge impact on your future success and happiness.

Here's why:

When you're young, you have a lot of time and energy to explore your interests and passions. By taking the time to get to know yourself, you can identify what you really enjoy and what you're good at. This can help you choose a career path or educational program that aligns with your interests and strengths, which can ultimately lead to a more fulfilling life.

Being comfortable with yourself at a young age can also help you build stronger relationships with friends, family, and romantic partners. When you're confident in who you are, you're more likely to attract positive people into your life who share your values and support your goals.

Investing in yourself is also crucial when you're young, as it can set you up for long-term success. For example, getting a college degree or learning a new skill can open up doors to new career opportunities and higher salaries. Pursuing hobbies and interests can also help you develop new talents and abilities that you can use to enhance your career or personal life.

Determining your objectives and lifestyle at a young age can help you stay focused and motivated as you work towards your goals. By setting specific, measurable goals and creating a plan to achieve them, you can stay on track and avoid getting sidetracked by distractions or setbacks.

Focusing on these four key areas of personal growth while you're young can help you build a strong foundation for a happy, successful life.

Step 2:

Understand the definitions and basics about:

Definitions and basics: Money, value, and rewards.

Money, value, and rewards are all important concepts that affect our daily lives. Money is what we use to buy the things we need or want, such as food, clothes, and entertainment. We work hard and earn money so that we can exchange it for the things we value.

Value refers to how much we think something is worth. We all have different opinions on what's valuable, and what we value can change over time. For example, when we're young, we may value having fun and hanging out with friends, but as we get older, we may value things like stability, security, and financial independence.

Rewards are the things we receive when we do something good or achieve a goal. For example, if we work hard and meet our sales targets, we may receive a bonus or recognition from our employer. Rewards can be both tangible, like money or a gift, and intangible, like praise or recognition.

Understanding the relationships between money, value, and rewards can help us make better decisions in our daily lives. We can prioritize the things we value most and work hard to earn the money we need to acquire them. We can also use rewards as motivation to achieve our goals and feel a sense of accomplishment when we succeed.

Money:

Money is what we use to buy the things we need and want, like food, clothes, and entertainment. It's like a special kind of token that we can exchange for goods and services. Money can be in different forms, like physical coins and banknotes, or digital forms like credit cards and electronic payments. Money is important because it's a widely accepted way to exchange value, and it helps us keep track of how much things are worth.

Cash is a type of money that we can hold in our hands. It includes physical currency, like bills and coins, that we can use to buy things in person. Cash is often preferred for small transactions, like buying a snack from a vending machine or paying a street vendor, because it's quick and easy. Plus, some people feel more secure when they can physically hold onto their money.

In business and investment, cash refers to the actual physical currency or funds that a company or individual has available for immediate use. It can also refer to assets that can be easily converted into cash, such as short-term investments or accounts receivable.

Having cash on hand is important for businesses, as it allows them to cover expenses like payroll, rent, and inventory purchases. Cash can also be used to take advantage of investment opportunities or to pay off debts.

Investors often look at a company's cash position when considering whether to invest in them. A healthy cash position can be a good sign that the company is financially stable and has the ability to invest in growth opportunities or return value to shareholders through dividends or share buybacks.

When it comes to understanding the value and worth of cash, it's important to consider both its immediate and long-term effects.

In the immediate sense, cash can provide immediate purchasing power and liquidity. It can be used to pay for goods and services, cover expenses, or invest in opportunities that arise. Having cash on hand can be important for emergencies or unexpected events that require quick access to funds.

However, in the long-term, the value of cash can corrode due to inflation. Inflation refers to the general increase in prices of goods and services over time, which reduces the purchasing power of money. This means that the same amount of cash will be able to buy fewer goods and services in the future than it can today.

Therefore, it's important to consider the long-term effects of holding onto cash and to ensure that it is invested in assets that can generate returns that outpace inflation over time. This can include investing in stocks, bonds, or real estate, which have historically provided returns that outpace inflation.

What is Value?

Value is a concept that refers to the worth, usefulness, or importance of something, whether it be an object, a service, time or an idea.

In economics, value can be defined as the amount of money that someone is willing to pay for something, based on their perception of its worth or usefulness.

Value is subjective, meaning that different people may assign different levels of value to the same thing based on their personal preferences, needs, and circumstances. For example, a piece of jewelry may have a high value to someone who considers it a family heirloom or a symbol of prestige, while it may have little or no value to someone who has no interest in jewelry or doesn't appreciate its aesthetic qualities. Value can be influenced by factors such as scarcity, quality, utility, brand recognition, and emotional attachment.

Recognizing the value of things is an important skill that can help you make better decisions when it comes to spending, investing, and managing your resources. To recognize the value of things, you need to consider various factors such as the utility or usefulness of the item, its quality, its uniqueness or rarity, its demand and availability, and its potential for appreciation or depreciation in value over time.

For example, when shopping for a car, you might consider the make and model, its features and performance, its reliability, fuel efficiency, and safety ratings, as well as its resale value. By evaluating these factors, you can determine the true value of the car and whether it's a good investment for your needs and budget.

Similarly, when considering investments, you might look at the current market trends, the company's financial health, its management team, and its competitive advantages to determine its potential for growth and profitability.

What is a reward?

A reward is something given or received in recognition of an action, effort, or achievement. Rewards can take many forms, such as money, gifts, prizes, recognition, or privileges, and they are often used to motivate or incentivize people to perform certain tasks, reach specific goals, or exhibit desired behaviors.

In psychology, rewards are a key component of operant conditioning, which is a type of learning that involves associating behaviors with their consequences. Positive reinforcement, or the provision of a reward for a desired behavior, is a powerful tool for shaping behavior and increasing the likelihood that it will be repeated in the future.

Rewards can also have a psychological impact, providing a sense of accomplishment, satisfaction, or validation. They can reinforce a person's self-esteem, confidence, and sense of competence, and they can contribute to feelings of happiness and well-being.

Rewarding yourself is a great way to celebrate your accomplishments and stay motivated to keep pushing forward. There are a lot of different ways you can reward yourself, depending on what you enjoy and what makes you feel good.

Here are a few ideas:

Treat yourself: This could be something you've been wanting for a while, like a new gadget, a piece of clothing, or a delicious treat. Whatever it is, it should be something that makes you feel happy and satisfied.

Take a break: Sometimes, the best way to reward yourself is by taking some time off to do something you enjoy. This could be anything from taking a walk in the park to binge-watching your favorite TV show.

Celebrate with loved ones: Sharing your accomplishments with friends or family is a great way to feel appreciated and recognized. You could invite them over for a meal or a get-together to celebrate your achievements together.

Treat yourself to self-care: Taking care of yourself is always a good way to reward yourself. This could be a spa day, a massage, or even just taking some time to read a book or meditate.

Acknowledge your hard work: Sometimes, the best reward is just acknowledging how hard you've worked and how much you've accomplished. Take a moment to reflect on your achievements and give yourself a pat on the back for a job well done.

Money vs Value?

Money and value are related concepts, but they are not the same thing. Money is a medium of exchange that people use to buy goods and services. It has no intrinsic value in and of itself, but rather it derives its value from the goods and services that it can be used to purchase.

Value, on the other hand, refers to the usefulness or importance of something, whether it is a good, a service, an asset, or an investment. Value is subjective and can be different for different people. For example, a painting may be valuable to a collector because of its historical significance, while it may have little value to someone who is not interested in art.

While money can be used to buy things of value, the two concepts are not interchangeable. For instance, a person may spend a large amount of money on something that they consider valuable, but others may not see the same value in it. Conversely, something may have a lot of value to someone, but may not require a large amount of money to acquire.

When it comes to time, money and value take on a different dimension. Time is a valuable and limited resource that cannot be replaced or replenished once it's gone. As a result, the way you spend your time can have a significant impact on your life, and how we perceive the value of money.

One way to think about the relationship between money, value, and time is to consider the concept of opportunity cost. Opportunity cost is the value of the next best alternative that you give up when you choose one option over another. For example, if you choose to spend an hour working, the opportunity cost is the value of the activities you could have done in that hour instead.

When it comes to money and value, the opportunity cost of spending money is the value of the things you could have done with that money instead. For instance, if you choose to spend money on an expensive car, the opportunity cost is the value of the things you could have done with that money, such as investing it, saving it, or using it to pursue other interests.

Therefore, it's important to consider the value of our time and the opportunity cost of our money when making decisions about how to spend them. This can help us make more informed choices that align with our values and priorities, and help us use our limited time and resources more effectively.

Money and time

Money and time are two of the most valuable resources we have, and they are often interconnected. Money can be earned, invested, and spent, while time is a finite resource that can never be regained once it's gone. The way we use our money and time can have a significant impact on our lives, and it's important to find a balance between the two.

Money can be used to buy time, or to create more time for ourselves. For example, we can hire someone to do tasks for us, such as cleaning our home, mowing our lawn, or running errands, freeing up our time to focus on other things. We can also use our money to invest in education or training that can improve our skills and increase our earning potential, allowing us to work more efficiently and effectively, and ultimately create more time for ourselves.

On the other hand, time can also be used to create wealth. By investing our time in activities that can generate income, such as starting a business, investing in real estate, or building a career, we can increase our earning potential and create financial security for ourselves.

However, it's important to find a balance between our time and money. We should not sacrifice our time at the expense of earning more money, as it can lead to burnout, stress, and a lack of fulfillment. Similarly, we should not prioritize our time at the expense of our financial well-being, as it can lead to financial insecurity and limit our opportunities.

The value of money and the value of time are two very different things, but they are both important in our lives. Money has a quantifiable value, meaning it can be measured in terms of its purchasing power, while time has an intangible value that is not so easily measured.

When we choose to spend money, we are essentially exchanging it for something of value, such as goods, services, or experiences. However, when we choose to spend time, we are giving up something that is irreplaceable and cannot be regained once it's gone. Therefore, the value of time is often considered more precious than the value of money.

In terms of personal fulfillment and satisfaction, the value of time often outweighs the value of money. For example, spending time with loved ones, pursuing a passion, or volunteering can provide a sense of purpose and fulfillment that money cannot buy. On the other hand, if we focus solely on the value of money, we may end up sacrificing our time and missing out on these valuable experiences.

However, it's important to note that money can also provide value in certain contexts. For instance, having financial stability and security can provide peace of mind and the ability to pursue our goals and dreams. Money can also be used to create opportunities and experiences that may not be possible otherwise.

Value and time

Value and time are closely linked concepts that play important roles in our lives. Value refers to the worth or usefulness of something, while time is the finite resource that we have to allocate to different activities.

When we make decisions about how to spend our time, we often consider the value of the activities we are choosing between. For example, we may choose to spend our time working on a project that has high value to us, such as pursuing a passion or working towards a long-term goal. Conversely, we may choose to avoid activities that have low value, such as mindlessly scrolling through social media or watching TV for hours on end. Similarly, when we invest our time in something, we are essentially giving it value. For example, the time we invest in building relationships with loved ones, pursuing education or training, or practicing a skill can increase their value to us over time. Conversely, neglecting these areas can result in a loss of value.

Value and time are also important factors to consider when making financial decisions. For example, investing in a quality product that lasts a long time can provide greater value than constantly replacing cheaper, lower-quality products. Similarly, investing in our education or skills can increase our earning potential over time, leading to greater financial value in the long run.

What is Saving:

Savings refers to the money that you set aside or keep aside for future use, rather than spending it immediately. Saving money is an important part of financial planning as it provides a safety net in case of unexpected expenses or emergencies, and helps you achieve your financial goals such as buying a home, starting a business, or retiring comfortably.

There are different types of savings, including short-term savings for emergencies or upcoming expenses, medium-term savings for specific goals such as a vacation or down payment on a house, and long-term savings for retirement. Saving money involves setting a budget and finding ways to reduce expenses, such as cutting back on unnecessary purchases or finding ways to save on regular bills.

One of the most effective ways to save money is to create a savings plan and automate your savings. This involves setting a specific savings goal, such as saving 10% of your income each month, and then setting up automatic transfers from your checking account to a savings account or investment account. By automating your savings, you can make sure that you are consistently saving money without having to think about it or actively make transfers.

Another important aspect of saving money is finding ways to make your savings work for you. This can involve researching different savings accounts, investment options, or retirement plans to find the best options for your financial goals and risk tolerance.

Saving and time are closely related concepts in personal finance. Time plays a critical role in how much you are able to save and the impact your savings have on your financial future.

One of the key factors that affects how much you can save is the amount of time you have to save. The longer you have to save, the more you can potentially accumulate in savings, as the power of compound interest increases the longer your money is invested.

For example, if you save $100 per month for 20 years, assuming an average annual rate of return of 7%, you would have over $44,000 in savings. However, if you saved the same amount for only 10 years, you would have less than half that amount, or around $18,000.

Another important aspect of saving and time is the concept of opportunity cost. Every dollar you spend today is a dollar that could have been invested or saved for the future. By prioritizing saving and investing over spending, you can take advantage of the power of compound interest and potentially achieve your financial goals more quickly.

Finally, time also plays a role in your ability to weather financial emergencies or unexpected expenses. By building an emergency fund and saving regularly, you can create a cushion that can help you manage unexpected expenses without having to rely on high-interest credit cards or other forms of debt.

Saving money is an important aspect of personal finance and can help you achieve a variety of financial goals.

Why to save:

Build an emergency fund: Saving money can help you prepare for unexpected expenses or emergencies.

Achieve financial goals: Saving money can help you reach specific financial goals such as buying a house, starting a business, or retiring comfortably.

Reduce debt: Saving money can help you pay off high-interest debt more quickly, reducing the amount of money you spend on interest over time. Build wealth: Saving and investing money can help you build long-term wealth and achieve financial freedom.

When to save:

Start early: The earlier you start saving, the more time you have to take advantage of compound interest and potentially build a larger nest egg.

Save regularly: Saving regularly, whether it's weekly, monthly, or annually, can help you build a consistent savings habit and make it easier to reach your financial goals.

Save when you have extra income: If you receive a bonus, tax refund, or other unexpected income, consider using some or all of it to boost your savings.

Where to save:

High-yield savings accounts: These accounts typically offer higher interest rates than traditional savings accounts, allowing you to earn more on your savings.

Investment accounts: Investing your savings can potentially earn higher returns over the long term, but also involves more risk.

Retirement accounts: Saving for retirement through a 401(k), IRA, or other retirement account can help you build a secure financial future.

How to save:

Create a budget: Understanding your income and expenses can help you identify areas where you can cut back and save more.

Automate your savings: Setting up automatic transfers from your checking account to a savings account or investment account can make it easier to save consistently.

Find ways to save on expenses: Look for ways to cut back on regular expenses such as housing, transportation, and food, and redirect those savings into your savings goals.

What is budget?

A budget is a financial plan that outlines how much money you expect to earn or receive, and how much you plan to spend or save over a certain period of time, typically a month or a year. The purpose of a budget is to help you manage your finances effectively, by tracking your income and expenses and ensuring that you are not overspending or living beyond your means.

Creating a budget involves several key steps. The first step is to determine your income, which can include your salary, any additional sources of income, and any benefits or allowances you receive. Once you have a clear picture of your income, you can then identify your expenses, which may include fixed expenses such as rent or mortgage payments, utilities, and insurance, as well as variable expenses such as groceries, transportation, and entertainment.

After identifying your income and expenses, you can then compare the two to determine whether you have a surplus or a deficit. If you have a surplus, you may want to consider saving or investing the extra money for future needs or goals. If you have a deficit, you may need to make adjustments to your expenses or find ways to increase your income, such as taking on additional work or negotiating a raise.

Budgeting requires discipline and commitment to sticking to your financial plan. It's important to track your expenses regularly, review your budget periodically to make any necessary adjustments, and prioritize your spending to ensure that you are meeting your financial goals.

Budget and time are two important resources that are closely interconnected. A budget involves managing your financial resources effectively, while time involves managing your available time to accomplish tasks and goals.

When it comes to budget and time management, it's important to create a realistic plan that takes into account both resources. For example, if you have a limited budget, you may need to allocate more time to researching deals or finding ways to save money. On the other hand, if you have a busy schedule, you may need to find ways to save time, such as outsourcing tasks or streamlining your daily routine, in order to avoid overspending.

One effective approach to managing both budget and time is to prioritize your goals and activities. By identifying the most important tasks and goals, you can allocate your resources accordingly and avoid wasting time or money on less important activities.

Another important aspect of budget and time management is tracking your progress and making adjustments as needed. For example, if you notice that you are consistently overspending in a certain category or failing to meet deadlines, you may need to adjust your budget or schedule to better align with your goals and priorities.

Credits, Loans, and Interest

Credit:

Credit refers to the ability to borrow money or obtain goods or services with the expectation of paying for them at a later time. When you use credit, you are essentially taking out a loan or making a purchase on credit, which you agree to pay back with interest or fees over time.

Credit can take many forms, including credit cards, personal loans, auto loans, mortgages, and student loans. In each case, the lender or creditor is providing you with money or goods based on the assumption that you will pay them back over time, typically with interest or fees.

However, it's important to use credit responsibly (if ever) and only borrow what you can afford to **repay back in full right away**, as failing to make payments on time or defaulting on a loan can have serious consequences for your credit score and financial future.

Your credit history, which includes your past use of credit and your ability to repay debts on time, is used by lenders and creditors to determine whether to approve you for credit in the future and what interest rates or fees to charge you. Maintaining a good credit history and credit score can help you access credit when you need it and save money on interest and fees over time.

Loans:

A loan is a type of financial transaction in which a lender provides money or other assets to a borrower, with the expectation that the borrower will repay the loan over time, typically with interest or fees.

There are many types of loans available, including personal loans, auto loans, mortgages, student loans, and business loans. The terms of a loan can vary widely, depending on the lender, the borrower's credit history and financial situation, and the purpose of the loan.

In most cases, when you take out a loan, you will need to sign a contract or agreement that outlines the terms of the loan, including the amount borrowed, the interest rate or fees, the repayment schedule, and any penalties for late or missed payments. It's important to read and understand the terms of the loan agreement before you sign, to ensure that you are comfortable with the terms and able to make the required payments on time.

Loans can be a useful tool for financing large purchases, such as a home or a car, or for investing in your education or business. However, it's important to use loans responsibly and only borrow what you can afford to repay, to avoid falling into debt or damaging your credit score.

If you are considering taking out a loan, it's a good idea to shop around and compare offers from different lenders to find the best terms and interest rates for your situation. You may also want to consider working with a financial advisor or credit counselor to help you make informed decisions about borrowing and managing your debt.

Loan Service fees:

Loan service fees are charges that a lender may impose on a borrower for processing and servicing a loan. These fees are usually separate from the interest rate and are intended to cover the administrative costs associated with managing the loan.
Common loan service fees include application fees, origination fees, and processing fees, which are charged when you first apply for the loan. Other fees, such as late payment fees, prepayment fees, or early termination fees, may be charged during the life of the loan if you fail to make payments on time or choose to pay off the loan early.

The amount of loan service fees that a lender charges can vary widely depending on the type of loan, the lender's policies, and the borrower's creditworthiness. Some lenders may charge a flat fee for each loan, while others may charge a percentage of the loan amount or interest rate.

It's important to read and understand the loan agreement before you sign, to ensure that you are aware of any loan service fees and other costs associated with the loan. You may also want to compare offers from multiple lenders to find the best terms and fees for your situation.

The cost of a loan includes the amount of money you borrow plus any interest, fees, or other charges associated with the loan. The total cost of the loan is typically expressed as the Annual Percentage Rate (APR), which includes both the interest rate and any fees or charges.

The cost of the loan can vary depending on a number of factors, including the type of loan, the lender, and your creditworthiness. Some loans, such as payday loans or high-interest credit cards, can have very high costs due to high interest rates and fees.

In addition to interest charges, lenders may also charge fees for processing and servicing the loan, such as application fees, origination fees, or late payment fees. These fees can add up quickly and increase the overall cost of the loan.

To understand the cost of a loan, it's important to read and understand the loan agreement, including the APR and any fees or charges associated with the loan. You may also want to compare offers from multiple lenders to find the best terms and rates for your situation. By understanding the cost of the loan, you can make informed decisions about borrowing and avoid taking on too much debt.

Interest:

Interest is the cost of borrowing money, typically expressed as a percentage of the amount borrowed. When you borrow money, you agree to pay back the principal amount plus interest over a specified period of time.

The interest rate can vary depending on a number of factors, including the type of loan, the lender, and your creditworthiness. Higher interest rates generally mean you will pay more over time, while lower interest rates can help you save money.

There are two types of interest: simple interest and compound interest. Simple interest is calculated based on the principal amount borrowed, while compound interest is calculated based on the principal amount plus any interest that has already accrued.

For example, if you borrow $1,000 at a 10% interest rate, you would owe $100 in interest for the first year ($1,000 x 0.10 = $100). With simple interest, you would owe $100 in interest each year, while with compound interest, you would owe interest on the original principal amount plus any interest that has already accrued.

When considering interest rates, it's important to understand the risks and potential downsides that come with borrowing money.

Here are some factors to consider:

Interest rates can change: Interest rates can fluctuate based on market conditions and other factors, which can impact the cost of borrowing. For example, if you have a variable-rate loan, your interest rate may increase over time, making your payments more expensive.

Higher interest rates can increase the cost of borrowing: When you borrow money, you agree to pay back the principal amount plus interest. Higher interest rates can increase the cost of borrowing, making it more difficult to pay off debt and potentially leading to financial stress.
Interest can compound: If you have a loan with compound interest, interest can accrue on the original principal amount plus any interest that has already accumulated. This can significantly increase the total amount you owe over time.

Default risk: If you are unable to make your loan payments on time, you may be subject to late fees or penalties, which can increase the cost of borrowing. If you default on the loan, your credit score may be negatively impacted and you may face legal action or collection efforts.

Opportunity cost: When you borrow money, you are essentially using future income to pay for something today. This means that you may be sacrificing future financial opportunities, such as saving for retirement or investing in a business, in order to pay off debt.

To mitigate these risks, it's important to carefully consider the terms and interest rate of any loan before borrowing, and to only borrow what you can afford to repay. You may also want to consider building an emergency fund and exploring other options for financing, such as grants, scholarships, or low-interest loans.

Investment

Investment refers to the act of putting money or resources into something with the expectation of earning a profit or gaining some other type of benefit. Typically, the goal of investing is to generate income or grow wealth over time.

There are many different types of investments, including stocks, bonds, real estate, and mutual funds. Each type of investment has its own risk profile, potential returns, and liquidity, and investors may choose to diversify their portfolio to reduce risk.

One key principle of investing is the tradeoff between risk and reward. Generally, investments with higher potential returns also come with higher levels of risk. Investors must carefully consider their risk tolerance and investment goals when deciding where to put their money.
Another important aspect of investing is the concept of compounding. By reinvesting earnings or dividends, investors can benefit from exponential growth over time. This means that even small investments made early on can compound to generate significant returns over a long period of time.

It's important to note that investing is not without risk, and there is no guarantee of returns. Investors should always do their due diligence, research potential investments thoroughly, and seek the advice of a financial professional before making any investment decisions.

There are several reasons why people choose to invest their money:

Potential for higher returns: Investing can provide the opportunity for higher returns than traditional savings accounts or other low-risk investments. While investing always carries some level of risk, many types of investments have historically provided greater returns over the long term.

Beat inflation: Inflation is the rate at which the general level of prices for goods and services is rising, which means that over time, the same amount of money can buy less. Investing can potentially help you beat inflation and maintain the purchasing power of your money.

Build wealth: Investing can help you build wealth over time. By starting early and consistently making contributions, you can take advantage of the power of compounding and potentially generate significant returns over the long term.

Meet financial goals: Investing can help you meet your financial goals, such as saving for retirement, paying for a child's education, or purchasing a home. By investing strategically, you can work towards achieving these goals more quickly and efficiently.

Diversification: Investing can provide diversification, which can help reduce risk. By spreading your money across different types of investments, you can potentially minimize the impact of any single investment performing poorly.

It's important to note that investing always carries some level of risk, and there is no guarantee of returns. Before making any investment decisions, it's important to carefully consider your goals, risk tolerance, and investment horizon, and to seek the advice of a financial professional.

Investing your money can offer many benefits. Firstly, it can potentially provide higher returns than keeping your money in a savings account, which can help grow your wealth over time. Secondly, it can help protect your money from the effects of inflation, which can erode the value of your savings over time.

Additionally, investing can help you reach your financial goals, such as saving for retirement, buying a home, or paying for your children's education. It can also provide diversification, which means spreading your money across different investments to minimize risk.

However, investing always carries some level of risk, so it's important to do your research, seek professional advice, and carefully consider your goals and risk tolerance before making any investment decisions.

Investing may seem like a daunting task, but it can be simplified into several steps. Firstly, you should identify your investment goals, such as saving for retirement, buying a house, or **building wealth**.

Next, you need to determine your risk tolerance, which refers to the amount of risk you're willing to take on to achieve your investment goals.

Then, you should choose an investment account that suits your needs, such as a brokerage account or retirement account. After that, it's time to research different investment options, such as stocks, bonds, mutual funds, or real estate, and create a diversified portfolio that spreads your investments across multiple asset classes to minimize risk.

It's important to regularly monitor and adjust your portfolio as needed, and seek professional advice from a financial advisor or broker to help you make informed decisions. Keep in mind that investing always involves some level of risk, so it's crucial to carefully consider your goals and risk tolerance before making any investment decisions.

Deciding when to invest depends on several factors, including:

Your financial goals: Your investment goals will determine your investment horizon. If your goals are long-term, you may be able to take on more risk and invest in stocks, while short-term goals may require more conservative investments such as bonds.

Market conditions: Market conditions can also play a role in when you choose to invest. If the market is experiencing a downturn, it may be a good time to invest as stock prices may be lower. Conversely, if the market is experiencing a bull run, you may want to exercise caution and consider waiting for a dip in prices before investing.

Your personal financial situation: Your personal financial situation, including your income, expenses, and debts, can also influence when you decide to invest. You may want to pay off high-interest debt before investing or build an emergency fund before committing to long-term investments.

Economic indicators: Economic indicators, such as inflation rates and interest rates, can also impact investment decisions. For example, if inflation is high, investing in stocks or other assets that appreciate in value can help you beat inflation.

Professional advice: It's always a good idea to seek the advice of a financial professional, such as a financial advisor or broker, who can provide guidance on investment strategies and help you make informed decisions. They can help you identify the best time to invest based on your goals and risk tolerance.

Step 3:

Realize the Power of time

The Power of time

The power of time is a significant factor in achieving success while still young. Young age provides individuals with better health, higher energy levels, greater availability, and more significant capacity to learn and take risks, making it an ideal time to pursue goals and dreams.

In addition to youth, having a strong passion and determination to achieve one's goals is also crucial. These traits provide individuals with the drive and motivation to persevere through challenges and setbacks, enabling them to continue moving forward and making progress towards their goals.

Investing time and effort into pursuits while young also allows individuals to develop their skills and capabilities, gaining valuable experience and knowledge that can set them up for greater success in the future. This is especially important in today's rapidly changing job market, where having a diverse set of skills and experience is highly valued.

Power of time is an incredible thing, especially when it comes to achieving our dreams and goals while we're young. You see, when we're young, we have more energy, better health, and more time to dedicate to the things that matter to us. Plus, we're often more eager and passionate about pursuing our dreams, which makes it easier to stay motivated even when we encounter obstacles or setbacks.

When we invest our time and effort into our passions and goals while we're still young, we're also able to develop our skills and capabilities. This experience and knowledge can then help us in the future, whether we're pursuing a career or starting our own business. Plus, by taking risks and trying new things while we're young, we're able to learn from our mistakes and develop resilience, which can also help us later on in life.

The power of time helps to achieve your financial goals over a longer period of time through consistent and disciplined investing. By starting early and investing consistently over time, you can take advantage of the power of time to achieve your financial goals, such as building wealth.

For example, consider two individuals who both want to save for retirement. One person starts investing at age 25 and invests consistently until age 65, while the other person waits until age 45 to start investing and invests the same amount each year until age 65. Assuming a 7% annual rate of return, the first person would have saved over $500,000 by age 65, while the second person would have saved only about $110,000.

This demonstrates the power of time in relation to capabilities. By starting early and investing consistently over a long period of time, individuals have the potential to achieve greater financial success and reach their financial goals more easily than those who wait and invest for a shorter period of time.

It's important to note that the power of time is not a guarantee of financial success, and investing always involves some degree of risk. It's important to conduct thorough research and seek the advice of a financial professional before making any investment decisions.

The power of time refers to the concept that the longer you hold onto an investment, the greater your potential returns can be. This is due to the effect of compounding, where the returns generated by an investment are reinvested and can generate additional returns in the future.

For example, if you invest $10,000 in a stock that generates an annual return of 8%, after one year you will have earned $800 in returns. If you reinvest that $800, your investment will be worth $10,800 at the end of year two. If you continue to reinvest your returns, your investment will grow exponentially over time.

The power of time also allows investors to ride out short-term market fluctuations and benefit from long-term growth trends. By investing early and allowing your investments to grow over time, you can potentially build a significant amount of wealth for the future.

However, it's important to note that investing always involves some degree of risk, and past performance is not indicative of future results. It's important to conduct thorough research and seek the advice of a financial professional before making any investment decisions.

For starters, when we're young, we have more energy, better health, and fewer responsibilities, which means we can dedicate more time and effort to the things that matter to us. We also have the ability to learn and absorb new information more quickly, which allows us to develop skills and knowledge that can serve us well in the future.

Moreover, being young can be a time of great creativity and exploration. It's a time when we're more likely to take risks, try new things, and pursue our passions without fear of failure. This mindset can be incredibly beneficial, as it allows us to discover new talents and interests, build resilience and confidence, and develop a sense of purpose and direction for our lives.

Another advantage of being young is the ability to form strong connections and relationships. Whether it's with family, friends, or romantic partners, the bonds we create when we're young can often last a lifetime and provide us with a sense of support, comfort, and belonging.

The Value of time when you are young:

Time is perhaps one of the most valuable resources you have while still young. It is a finite resource that we cannot get back once it has passed, which is why it is important to use it wisely. The value of time lies in the fact that it allows us to accomplish our goals, pursue our passions, and live a fulfilling life.

Time is a commodity that is equally available to everyone, regardless of their background or resources. It is up to us to decide how we use this time, and what we choose to prioritize. By investing our time in things that matter to us, we can create a life that is meaningful and fulfilling.

Time also provides us with the opportunity to learn, grow, and develop as individuals. Whether it's by reading books, pursuing new hobbies, or taking courses, time allows us to acquire knowledge and skills that can enhance our lives and help us achieve our goals.

Moreover, time is essential for building relationships and connecting with others. It allows us to spend quality time with our loved ones, build strong connections with colleagues and friends, and create a sense of community and belonging.

The value of time in regards to money is significant. Time is a valuable resource that cannot be bought or sold. However, time is required to make money, and the amount of time invested can have a direct impact on the amount of money earned.

Time can also be a factor in the growth and sustainability of investments. The longer an investment has to grow, the more time it has to accumulate compound interest and appreciate in value.

On the other hand, time can also be a cost, as the longer it takes to earn money, the more opportunities there are for expenses and inflation to erode the purchasing power of that money. Therefore, managing time effectively is crucial in making the most of financial opportunities and achieving financial goals.

Time and Money:

Time can decrease the value of money due to inflation. Inflation is the gradual increase in prices of goods and services over time, which means that the same amount of money can buy less in the future than it can today.

For example, if the inflation rate is 2% per year, then in 10 years, the purchasing power of $100 will decrease to about $82. Therefore, if you save money for a long time without investing it in assets that can keep up with or outpace inflation, you risk losing the value of that money over time.

This is why it's important to invest in assets that can generate a return that is higher than the rate of inflation, such as stocks, real estate, or bonds. By doing so, you can protect the purchasing power of your money and potentially grow your wealth over time.

Time and Investment value:

Time can increase the value of your investment through the power of compound interest. Compound interest is the interest earned on both the principal amount and the interest already earned.

This means that over time, your investment can grow at an exponential rate, as the interest earned on your initial investment is reinvested to earn even more interest.

For example, if you invest $10,000 in a stock with an annual return of 8%, after one year, your investment would be worth $10,800. If you reinvest the $800 earned in interest and the stock continues to earn 8% each year, after 10 years, your investment would be worth over $21,500.

This is because the interest earned in the first year earns interest in the following years, resulting in a snowball effect that can significantly increase the value of your investment over time.

Therefore, the longer you invest your money, the more time it has to grow and compound, potentially resulting in a much larger return on your initial investment. This is why it's important to start investing as early as possible and to stay invested for the long term, allowing time to work in your favor to increase the value of your investment.

Time and Interest:

Time can increase the cost of loans, credit, and interest rates because of the concept of compounding interest. The longer you take to pay off a loan or credit, the more interest will accumulate over time, resulting in a higher overall cost.

Similarly, when borrowing money, the longer the repayment term, the higher the interest rate tends to be, which can result in a higher cost of borrowing. This is why it is important to pay off loans and credit as quickly as possible to minimize the impact of compounding interest and reduce the overall cost.

When you borrow money from a lender, they charge you interest as a fee for borrowing their money. This interest rate is usually expressed as an annual percentage rate (APR), and it is the cost of borrowing money over a period of time.

The longer you take to repay the loan, the more interest will accrue, increasing the overall cost of the loan. This is because interest is typically calculated on the remaining balance of the loan, so the longer it takes to pay it off, the more interest will accumulate.

The same concept applies to credit cards. If you carry a balance on your credit card and only make the minimum payment each month, interest will continue to accrue on the remaining balance, which can quickly add up over time. This is why it's important to pay off credit card debt as quickly as possible to avoid paying unnecessary interest charges.

On the other hand, when you invest your money, time can work in your favor by allowing your investments to grow and compound over time. The longer your money stays invested, the more time it has to grow and potentially earn a higher return.

This is why it's important to start investing as early as possible, as even small amounts of money can grow significantly over time through the power of compound interest.

The theory of "Everything now" suggests that we should prioritize efficiency and productivity by multitasking and doing everything at once, while the theory of "One thing at a time" suggests that we should focus on completing one task at a time in a deliberate and focused manner.

The proponents of the "Everything now" theory argue that modern life is fast-paced and demands that we juggle multiple tasks simultaneously. They believe that multitasking can increase efficiency and productivity because we can accomplish more in less time.

On the other hand, supporters of the "One thing at a time" theory argue that multitasking can actually decrease productivity and increase stress. They believe that by focusing on one task at a time, we can give it our full attention and complete it more effectively and efficiently. They also argue that multitasking can lead to mistakes and errors, which can ultimately cost more time and resources in the long run.

In reality, both theories have their merits, and the best approach may depend on the specific task and individual preferences. Some tasks may require multitasking, such as responding to emails while on a conference call, while others may require a more focused approach, such as writing an important report.

Ultimately, the key is to find a balance between the two approaches that works best for the individual and the task at hand. It's important to be mindful of how we approach our work and to be willing to adjust our strategies as needed to maximize efficiency and productivity.

The journey to becoming Rich

Now that we have established the foundation of personal and psychological development required for building wealth, it's time to move forward to the next step. This may involve acquiring new skills, networking with other successful individuals, and identifying opportunities for growth and investment.

Building wealth is not a one-time event, but rather a continuous process that requires ongoing effort and dedication. By staying focused on your goals and remaining committed to the process, you can continue to improve your financial situation and achieve long-term success.

Remember, success is not just about financial gain, but also about personal growth and fulfillment. By maintaining a positive mindset and cultivating healthy habits, you can build the foundation for a fulfilling and prosperous life.

Becoming wealthy

Becoming wealthy doesn't require any secret strategies, but rather a series of small actions, disciplined habits, and a willingness to begin managing your finances.

Starting the journey towards financial success is more important than striving for perfection. Many people feel overwhelmed and believe that they need to be financial experts to manage their money effectively, leading them to avoid taking any action.
Thus, the simplest approach to managing your money is to take it step-by-step and not worry about achieving absolute perfection.

Building wealth and becoming financially successful does not require a complex strategy or magical formula. In fact, the path to success is quite straightforward: **To achieve financial success, it's crucial to maintain a balance between income and expenses. This means that you should aim to earn more than you spend and try to save as much as you can.**

However, it can be challenging to execute this plan in a world where student loans, rising costs of living, inflation, and unexpected financial emergencies are all too common. Despite these challenges, it's possible to overcome obstacles and achieve financial security.

Saving money is just the first step towards financial success. Once you have built up your savings, it's important to make your money work for you by investing it wisely.

Investing can help your savings grow over time and generate additional income, allowing you to achieve your financial goals more quickly. However, it's important to remember that investing carries some degree of risk and requires careful research and planning to ensure that you are making sound financial decisions.

Step 4

TE-SIDE

Set objectives for your finances

Eliminate your debts completely

Build up an emergency fund

Commence your investment journey immediately

Broaden your investment portfolio

Increase your earnings

Step 4 consists of: TE-SIDE

Target

Eliminate Debt

Save

Invest

Diversify

Extra Income

TE-SIDE:

- Target:

Establish Financial Goals: Establishing financial goals is crucial for long-term success. It's important to have a clear understanding of what you want to achieve and create a plan to get there. Financial goals can include saving for a down payment on a house, creating a retirement fund, paying off debt, or saving for a child's education.

Here are some examples of specific financial goals:

- Save $20,000 for a down payment on a house within the next two years
- Pay off $10,000 in credit card debt within the next year
- Contribute $5,000 per year to a retirement account
- Save $10,000 for a child's college education within the next five years

- Eliminate Debt

Destroy Your Debt: Debt can be a significant obstacle to achieving financial success. High-interest debt, such as credit card debt, can quickly accumulate and lead to financial stress. To "destroy" your debt, it's important to create a plan to pay it off as quickly as possible.

Here are some strategies for paying off debt:

- Create a budget and prioritize debt payments
- Consider consolidating high-interest debt into a lower-interest loan
- Use the debt avalanche or debt snowball method to focus on paying off one debt at a time
- Avoid taking on new debt while paying off existing debt

- **S**ave:

Create a Cushion: Creating a cushion, or emergency fund, is important for unexpected expenses such as car repairs, medical bills, or job loss. Ideally, an emergency fund should cover three to six months' worth of living expenses.

Here are some tips for creating an emergency fund:

- Set a savings goal and make regular contributions
- Consider keeping your emergency fund in a separate account from your other savings
- Prioritize creating an emergency fund over other financial goals until you have a sufficient cushion
- **I**nvest

Start Investing Now: Investing is crucial for long-term financial success. The earlier you start investing, the more time your money has to grow.

Here are some examples of investment options:

- Retirement accounts.

- Mutual funds or exchange-traded funds.
- Individual stocks or bonds.
- Real estate investments

- **D**iversify

Diversify Your Portfolio: Diversifying your portfolio means spreading your investments across multiple asset classes, industries, and geographic regions. This can help reduce risk and maximize returns.

Here are some tips for diversifying your portfolio:

- Consider investing in a mix of stocks, bonds, and cash equivalents
- Invest in companies across different industries and sectors
- Consider international investments to diversify geographically
- Boost Your Income: Increasing your income can help you achieve your financial goals more quickly.

- **E**xtra Income:

Boost Your Income: Increasing your income can help you achieve your financial goals more quickly.

Here are some strategies for boosting your income:

- Negotiate a raise at your current job
- Take on a side hustle or freelance work
- Consider starting a business or investing in rental property
- Invest in yourself by learning new skills or pursuing advanced education

Build Your Career

1. How to Build Your Career and Increase Your Earnings

Building your career can help you increase your earnings potential.

Here are a few ways to do it:

- Get educated or seek training to develop new skills. A college degree or vocational training can help you stand out to potential employers.
- Find a mentor who can teach you valuable career skills.
- When you feel like you deserve a raise, ask for one! Document your successes and achievements to show your employer why you're an asset.

2. Supplement Your Income with a Second Job or Side Hustle

If your first job isn't paying enough, consider getting a second income stream or starting a side hustle. Here are a few ideas:

- Look for a part-time job or freelance work.
- Use your skills and talents to start a side hustle doing odd jobs, taking art commissions, or delivering food.

3. Choose a Career with Good Salary Prospects

Choosing a career with high earning potential can help you get rich. Here are a few examples of careers that typically pay well:

- Doctors, surgeons, and anesthesiologists typically have large salaries.
- Engineers who work with gas and oil companies can make a good living.
- Lawyers and IT managers/software engineers can also make a lot of money.

4. Grow Your Career by Finding New Jobs and Employers

Once you have some experience, consider finding a new, better-paying job in the same industry. Here are a few tips:

- Look for entry-level jobs at companies that promote internally.
- Consider moving to a city with more job opportunities.
- Stick with your current job if you're comfortable, but don't be afraid to look for something better.

Saving Money & Cutting Costs

Saving money and becoming rich is a goal many people aspire to achieve. It takes discipline, dedication, and hard work.

1. **Set financial goals and decide how much you want to save.**

   The first step to saving money is making a plan. Start by asking yourself questions to determine your exact financial goals. When do you want to retire? Are you saving up for things like a family or a child? What do you want to do once you're wealthy?

   Set your goals and figure out roughly how much money you need to save to fulfill your idea of "rich." When determining how much money you want to accumulate, be sure to make an emergency fund one of your goals if you don't already have one.

   Emergency funds typically equal 3 to 6 months of living expenses. Should anything happen, like the loss of a job or a medical emergency, they allow you to pay for what you need without experiencing financial turmoil.

2. **Save 15% of your annual gross income.**

   Every time you get paid, put a chunk of money into your savings and don't touch it. Calculate 15% of each paycheck and commit to saving that amount every time you're paid. Then, see if you can start saving even more as time goes on; 15% is a good minimum, but 20% of your total income is an even better goal.

Getting rich usually isn't an immediate process; it's the result of dedicating saving, budgeting, and investing. **The more you save now, the more you'll have later!**

3. **Make a monthly budget and stick to it diligently.**

    Create a monthly budget that covers all of your basic expenses and planned savings as illustrated above while leaving a little bit of "fun" money aside if possible.

    Sticking by your budget and saving at least some money each month is a good way to lay the groundwork for your efforts to get rich! Try using a budgeting app like Mint or Everydollar to build a budget.

4. **Keep track of all your expenses to save money efficiently**.

    Tracking your expenses is crucial to cutting costs efficiently and adhering to your monthly budget. The closer you monitor your personal spending, the easier it'll be to stick to the budget and build your wealth! Pick an expense-tracking app (Mint and Everydollar can also do this) and record every single cent that goes in and out of your wallet.

    After 3 months or so, you'll be able to find out where most of your money goes and where you can make it go even further.

5. **Get rid of all your debts and commit to staying debt-free**.

    Debt will keep draining your money as you make it, making it pretty hard to get rich as long as you have any debt attached to your name.

    If you have any debt, make paying it off one of your top financial priorities. Once you're debt-free, do your best to stay that way for the foreseeable future! Try to use cash (or debit) more than you use a credit card.

People who use credit cards for purchases often end up spending more money, and it's easy to get into debt if you can't pay off your card every month. If you do keep using a credit card regularly, try to pay off the full balance each month on time to gain interest-free credit and avoid late fees. Consider refinancing your home if you have a large 30-year mortgage, take on a 15-year mortgage instead. That way, you can pay off your debt faster and save money by paying fewer interest fees.

6. Look for ways to reduce your living expenses and save Money

It's no secret that living expenses can add up quickly. Whether you're trying to save money for a big purchase, pay off debt, or just want to be more financially responsible, reducing your living expenses can be a great way to achieve your goals. The good news is that there are plenty of ways to cut costs in your everyday life without sacrificing too much.

One of the simplest ways to reduce your living expenses is to look for corners you can cut. For example, try to eat out less often and cook more meals at home. You might be surprised at how much money you can save by doing this. Saving a few bucks here and there might not feel like "getting rich," but it'll absolutely make a difference in the long run. The money adds up, which is why even small changes to your spending habits can lead to significant savings over time.

If you're looking for more dramatic ways to reduce your living expenses, consider downsizing your car or house. For example, you might be able to make do with an apartment instead of a house or buy a used car instead of a new one. These changes might take some getting used to, but they can save you a lot of money in the long run.

Another easy way to reduce your living expenses is to avoid spending money on things you don't need. For example, if you're in the habit of stopping at Starbucks every morning for a $4 designer coffee, consider making coffee at home instead. That $4 might not seem like much, but it adds up quickly. If you skip Starbucks every weekday for a year, you'll save $1,460. That's a significant amount of money that you could put toward your financial goals instead.

7. Living a modest lifestyle

Living a modest lifestyle might not sound like the most glamorous way to get rich, but it's one of the easiest ways to maintain wealth and achieve financial stability over time. As you start earning more money, it's tempting to start spending more on luxuries and living a more extravagant lifestyle. However, the key to building wealth is to resist that urge and continue saving and investing more.

When you start accumulating more money from your career, savings, and investments, it's easy to fall into the trap of spending more than you should. It's important to be mindful of your spending habits and to avoid making impulsive purchases that could ultimately harm your long-term financial health.

For example, let's say you're currently living in a great apartment in a nice part of town, paying $1,200 each month in rent. If you suddenly start earning more money, you might be tempted to upgrade to a more expensive apartment that costs $1,600 per month. But do you really need to do that? Is it necessary to spend an extra $400 each month just because you can afford to?

Living a modest lifestyle means being content with what you have and being mindful of your spending habits. It doesn't mean you can't enjoy the fruits of your labor, but it does mean being thoughtful about when you're spending money because you can and when it's really necessary.

By living within your means, you can avoid getting into debt and accumulating unnecessary expenses. Instead, you can focus on building wealth over time by saving and investing more of your income.

You can also take advantage of opportunities to reduce your expenses and save money, such as cutting back on eating out, downsizing your car or house, and reducing your utility bills.

8. Be wise with your spending by making smart choices and avoiding financial mistakes

Making smart financial decisions is crucial to building and maintaining a stable financial future. It can be challenging to make ends meet, especially when you are spending your hard-earned cash on things that don't matter or won't help you get ahead. Therefore, it is crucial to reevaluate the things you spend money on and learn to manage your money wisely.

One of the essential steps towards financial success is figuring out when something is genuinely worth it and when it is frivolous spending. For instance, gambling in casinos and buying lottery tickets are statistically unlikely to help you get rich but are more likely to drain your wallet over time. It is vital to avoid these financial black holes that can lead to long-term financial difficulties.

Another common mistake people make is spending money on luxurious items like a first-class plane ticket. Although it is comfortable, it may not be worth the extra $1,000 or more. You can still reach your destination just as well in coach, and you can save that extra money for other essential expenses.

It is also essential to avoid making purchases that depreciate rapidly, such as buying a new car worth $50,000 or more. Such purchases can be a waste of money because they will not be worth half that much in five years. Instead, consider buying a cheaper car that can serve you just as well and be more financially efficient.

Investing Money Wisely

As the world continues to evolve and the economy changes, there is no guaranteed way to become wealthy overnight, there are several avenues millennials can explore to increase their wealth.

Becoming a realtor is one of the quickest and most lucrative ways for millennials to generate wealth fast. According to Marcus P. Miller, CFP, a financial advisor at Mainstay Capital, one can become a licensed real estate agent by completing their state's required pre-licensing education, passing their state's licensing exam, and then getting hired or joining a brokerage.

As a realtor, one can make money quickly by selling homes and collecting commission.

Starting a digital company, taking on freelance work, becoming a consultant, or offering coaching services are also great ways for millennials to generate wealth quickly. By identifying their skills or expertise, they can market their services through social media and other platforms to find clients who are willing to pay for their services.

Starting a small business is another option for millennials looking to generate wealth quickly. They can start a business in any field and start earning money as soon as they get their business up and running.

Jumping on the short-term rental trend is also a great way to generate income. With travel continuing to expand post-pandemic, short-term rentals through sites like Airbnb and VRBO are becoming more popular. Renting out a room or property on these platforms can bring in a significant income.

Investing in real estate is another option that millennials can explore. With high inflation and high-interest rates, most investments are expensive and offer limited quick returns. However, residential rental properties offer a higher value floor and excellent resilience during high inflation, making them a good investment choice.

Lastly, **seeking professional advice** from a financial advisor can help millennials make more confident decisions about managing their money and future investments. Financial advisors can provide personalized advice and guidance, working with millennials to make a plan to achieve their unique financial goals and prepare them for the unexpected.

To Be Rich

What Does It Mean To Be Rich? Tips and Insights from Finance Experts
When you think of the word "rich", what comes to mind? Perhaps a luxurious lifestyle filled with exotic cars, designer clothes, and private jets? While those things may be associated with wealth, being rich means much more than just material possessions.

According to Andrew Lokenauth, CEO of Fluent in Finance LLC, being rich means having time and location freedom to do the things that matter to you. In other words, being rich is about having the flexibility to live life on your own terms.

But how do you get there? Many finance experts agree that wealth often comes first from being frugal. Kyle Kroeger, finance expert at The Impact Investor, expands the definition of rich to mean "someone (who) regularly earned enough to be far from troubled paying their fixed expenses such as rent, electricity and other utilities, car maintenance costs, health insurance and educational expenses."

So, **how can you start building wealth and achieving financial freedom**?

Pay Off Debt: Debt can hold you back from achieving your financial goals. "If you're looking to get rich, stop carrying so much credit card debt," advises Matt Dixon, RFC partner and financial advisor at TruNorth Advisors.

"You need to organize your debt and start attacking the lowest balance first by paying as much as you can on that card all while maintaining minimum payments on your other cards. This doesn't mean you should never use a credit card, but make sure you use it responsibly and make your monthly payments."

Watch Your Risk: Be selective about the opportunities you are going after. "Wealthy people try not to take on too much risk and are very detail-oriented," says Dixon. Make sure your portfolio is diverse. Try investing in real estate or land. A diverse portfolio can help you hedge against the ups and downs of the market."

Start Your Own Company and Sell It Later: If you've got an entrepreneurial spirit, consider starting a company you can sell for bigger bucks, says Jared Bauman, co-founder and CEO of 201 Creative LLC, a digital marketing agency. "To be more successful," he said, "it is preferable to come up with an innovative solution to a specific problem in the market and start a business around it. ... However, if you succeed, you'll reap enormous rewards. This is a common practice among wealthy individuals."

Participate in a Startup and Receive Stock: Startups still abound, and they're always seeking new blood. "If you can acquire equity positions in one or more start-up companies, you could make a significant monetary gain if the company thrives and either floats or is sold to a larger enterprise," said Daniel Carter, SEO manager of Skuuudle.

Focus On Your Retirement Plan: Retirement accounts, which are typically invested in the stock market and thus more likely to earn good returns, are a good way to build wealth for later on. "If your employer has a retirement savings program for employees, make an effort to contribute to it," said Francis Locknear, founder of TheCostGuys.com. "Employers will contribute to retirement plans the same amount that you contribute toward your account. You can consider an RSP/RRSP if your employer doesn't offer you a retirement plan."

Try Affiliate Marketing: Affiliate marketing is a way for website owners, social media "influencers", and bloggers to promote a third-party product by providing a link to it on their site or social media account. This earns you income that can add up over time, says Adam Wood, co-founder of RevenueGeeks. "Although Amazon is the most well-known affiliate partner, other

Additionally, being rich does not necessarily mean having an exorbitant amount of money in your bank account. It is also about having financial security and stability. According to financial expert Kyle Kroeger, someone who regularly earns enough to cover their fixed expenses such as rent, utilities, car maintenance costs, health insurance, and educational expenses can also be considered rich.

For those looking to increase their wealth, financial advisor Matt Dixon advises paying off credit card debt and organizing debt to start attacking the lowest balance first, all while maintaining minimum payments on other cards. This helps to eliminate debt, which can be a major roadblock to becoming rich.

However, it is also important to be mindful of risk when investing. Wealthy people try not to take on too much risk and are very detail-oriented. It is crucial to be selective about the investment opportunities you are going after and to ensure that your portfolio is diverse to hedge against the ups and downs of the market. Investing in real estate or land is also a viable option for building wealth.

Entrepreneurship is another avenue for building wealth, as starting a company and selling it later can reap enormous rewards. Co-founder and CEO of 201 Creative LLC, Jared Bauman, suggests that to be more successful, it is preferable to come up with an innovative solution to a specific problem in the market and start a business around it.

For those who do not want to start their own company, participating in a **startup** and receiving stock is another option. While it is a small number of startups that succeed on a large scale, early employees at Apple, Google, and Microsoft became millionaires on this basis.

Retirement accounts are also a good way to build wealth for later on. Contributing to your employer's retirement savings program and considering an IRA if your employer does not offer a retirement plan can set you on the path to financial stability in your later years.

Affiliate marketing is another way to earn income over time. Website owners, social media influencers, and bloggers use affiliate marketing to promote third-party products by providing a link to it on their site or social media account. This can add up over time and is seen as a passive way to earn money.

Investing in real estate investment trusts (*REITs*) can also be a way to build wealth. REITs allow investors to own and manage property and pay minimal or no corporate income tax if they distribute the majority of their profits to shareholders. The best REITs have a track record of increasing their payout on an annual basis, providing investors with a steady stream of dividends over time.

Step 5

THE PLAN
And The Bottom Line

THE PLAN

And The Bottom Line

Being Rich is a dream for many, but it requires careful planning and disciplined saving. In this final chapter, we'll outline a six-step plan to help you get there while still young.

Step #1: Rethink Your Lifestyle

The first step to be rich by 45 is to reevaluate your lifestyle. Unless you're earning a very high income, you may have to adjust your spending habits to achieve your goal. Start by reviewing your budget and identifying any nonessential spending.

Eliminating non-mortgage debt, such as student loans, credit cards, and car loans, can also help. Becoming rich will require sacrificing some luxuries, such as eating out or engaging in hobbies.

Cutting these expenses may seem small, but they can make a big difference in reaching your goal. Ultimately, you'll need to save more aggressively and invest more tactically to retire early. The money you save by age 45 will have to sustain you for the rest of your life.

Step #2: Get Clear on Your Vision

Next, define what "rich" means to you. Maybe it involves traveling, exploring new hobbies, starting a business, or even going back to school, or simply not to have to work a full time job anymore. The possibilities are limitless, but you'll need to understand how much your vision will cost to develop a plan to get there.

Creating an estimated budget will help you avoid shortfalls. Include all your basic living expenses, and then add in other costs that you may have to adjust for as you get older, such as paying for your children's education or rising health care expenses.

A savings calculator can help you determine how much you need to reach your goal.

Step #3: Accelerate Your Income

Most people enter their peak earning years in their 40s and 50s. If you're planning to retire by then, you may need to pick up the pace with your earnings now. You could ask for a promotion or raise at your current job or **take on a part-time job**. If those aren't options, consider starting a **side hustle** or a **small business** to increase your earnings. Use this extra stream of income to invest it and make this income work for you by re-investing it all.

The higher your income, the more you can save. Focus on increasing contributions to your **investment accounts** rather than living more lavishly as you earn a higher salary.

Step #4: Invest Strategically

Investing experts agree that the younger you are, the more risk you can afford to take on. But getting rich while you are still young will add a wrinkle to that logic. If you know you want to be rich by 45, you may want to take a more conservative approach so as not to jeopardize your plan.

When adding investments to your portfolio, be sure to diversify. Also, factor in the fees you're paying for each investment. Fees can nibble away at your returns over time, so you should minimize them wherever possible.

Step #5: Manage Your Tax Liability

Investing means periodic rebalancing to stay on track with your performance goals and tax loss harvesting. Loss harvesting means selling an asset that's declined in value to counter the capital gains tax you might pay on a different investment that's performed well.

Take advantage of tax-advantaged accounts. With traditional plans and RSP's, your contributions are generally tax-deductible and withdrawals are taxed in retirement at your ordinary income tax rate. You can also take advantage of the increasing new home production and doubling the first-time homebuyer's credit, they've introduced a new way to save up to $40,000 on your first home tax-free called the Tax-Free First Home Savings Account (FHSA).

Step #6: Get Professional Help

Consider consulting with a financial advisor. An experienced advisor can help you set realistic goals, identify the right investments, and make sure you stay on track.

Choose a fiduciary advisor who is legally bound to act in your best interests. You can find an advisor through professional organizations such as the National Association of Personal Financial Advisors or the Financial Planning Association.

Make sure to ask about the advisor's experience and fee structure before hiring them.

Step #7: Stay Focused

Getting rich takes discipline and focus. You'll need to stick to your budget, save aggressively, and invest wisely.

It may also require some sacrifice in the short-term, such as putting off major purchases or living below your means.

Staying focused on your goals can help you resist temptation and stay on track. Consider creating a vision board or using other tools to stay motivated.

It's also important to stay informed about changes in tax laws, investment strategies, and other factors that can impact your plans.

Final Thoughts

Becoming rich at 45 is a lofty goal, but it's not impossible. It requires careful planning, diligent saving and investing, and a willingness to adjust your lifestyle. With the right strategy and discipline, you can enjoy a fulfilling lifestyle at an early age.

Remember to seek professional advice if needed, stay focused on your goals, and stay informed about changes in the financial landscape.

Most importantly, don't lose sight of the bigger picture:

The freedom and flexibility to live the life you want, on your own terms.

Final Word

As a parent, I have always been concerned about my children's financial future. I wanted to make sure they have the tools and knowledge necessary to build a solid financial structure and develop wise money manners while they are young, so they can succeed in their financial endeavors in the future.

Through my own experience and research, I have learned that developing good financial habits is essential to achieving financial independence and security.

But I also realized that many young people today lack the necessary financial education and guidance to make informed decisions about their money.

That's why I wrote this book. It is my hope that by sharing my insights and experiences, I can help my children and other young readers build a strong foundation for their financial future.

In this book, I covered a range of topics, from budgeting and saving to investing and entrepreneurship. I offered practical advice and tips, as well as personal narratives to illustrate the importance of each topic.

I believe that financial education should be a priority for all young people, and I hope this book will inspire and empower readers to take control of their financial lives.

My advice

As a parent, I want you to know that one of the most important things you can do for yourself is to build a strong financial foundation. Money can be a powerful tool when used wisely, but it can also be a source of stress and worry if mismanaged.

I know you are young, but it's never too early to start learning about money and how to make it work for you. By developing good habits now, you can set yourself up for a bright financial future.

Here are some tips that I hope will help you along the way:

1. Always live within your means. Spend less than you earn, and avoid taking on unnecessary debt.
2. Save regularly. Whether it's setting aside a portion of your allowance or earning money from a part-time job, make a habit of putting money aside for the future.
3. Invest wisely. Learn about different investment options, and choose ones that align with your financial goals and risk tolerance.
4. Be charitable. Giving back to those in need can be a rewarding experience, and can also help you learn about the importance of generosity.
5. Practice good manners. Always be polite and respectful when dealing with others, especially when it comes to money.

Remember, building a strong financial foundation takes time and effort, but it's worth it in the end. I believe in you, and know that with hard work and dedication, you can achieve anything you set your mind to.

References

Jared Bauman, co-founder and CEO of 201 Creative LLC , a digital marketing agency.

Daniel Carter, SEO manager of Skuuudle

Francis Locknear, founder of TheCostGuys.com

www.ingramcontent.com/pod-product-compliance
Lightning Source LLC
Chambersburg PA
CBHW071045220526
45467CB00004B/1678